BEAUTIFUL CONSCIOUS LOVE
The Poetry of Kimeko Farrar
Vol. 1

By Kimeko Farrar

Foreword by Marc Lacy

ChUC, ink
2013

BEAUTIFUL CONSCIOUS LOVE: THE POETRY OF KIMEKO FARRAR.

ISBN-13: 978-0-9893715-0-6

Copyright © 2013 by Kimeko Farrar.

All rights reserved.

No part of this book may be used or reproduced in any manner whatsoever without written permission except in the case of brief quotations embodied in critical articles or reviews.

Printed in the United States of America.

COVER DESIGN by charlesbeason.net

www.kimekofarrar.com

Farrar, Kimeko, 1973-

Beautiful Conscious Love

A beautiful spirit is woven from a delicate pattern of pain, joy, and talents

Far from pure

But it can be seen

Even through Lyrca laced fabrics and ruby red lips

If you look for it

It is conscious

It has a conscience

And a kind heart that bleeds for other people's sorrow

And makes pretty stains on the world

It wants to heal and be healed

So the beautiful spirit loves

Loves hard

Loves crazy

Loves deep

'Cause it can't stop feeling

Can't stop growing

Can't stop acknowledging

That as long as it shines

There is hope

~ Kimeko Farrar

Foreword

When I hear the name Kimeko Farrar, a wide spectrum of things comes to mind. However, there's no paragraph or article long enough to accommodate all of what could be said about this fascinating young lady. Not even the National Weather Service could forecast how Kimeko Farrar would storm onto the national spoken word scene. Athens, Alabama was the genesis of this bona fide #chickundercontstruction who is not through making her mark. Deep country born, humbly bred, and engineer educated, the depth of loyalty within her friendship is immeasurable. Kimeko makes it easy for one to call her a friend. This is why so many are ecstatic about the harvest of blessings that are manifesting themselves in her life. Never have the masses witnessed such a positive and motley mixed blessing from the recipes of God Almighty. She is a brilliant writer and poet whose work is sprinkled with a beautiful personality fueled by a big selfless heart. Her soul piercing words are launched from a face of splendor that's gift wrapped by a richly natural mane, sitting atop the epitome of a queenly-endowed anatomy. Kimeko is like a kaleidoscope of colorful country cuteness with just enough of a southern fried edge. So keep your eyes focused on center stage as she delivers a dose of lyrical hypnotic medicine in a digestible fashion...with an enlightening side effect.

Whether it is meant for you to understand every aspect of her or not, three things are unmistakable. Kimeko is BEAUTIFUL, Kimeko is CONSCIOUS, and Kimeko is LOVE.

Poet/Author Marc Lacy

Table of Contents

Chapter I: Beautified
- BADD Chick 2
- Black Girls Rock 4
- Look at Me 6
- Make Me Over 7
- Naturalista 9
- Social Media 11
- Shoe Game 12
- Black Doll 13
- First Lady 15
- Girls and Pigtails 16
- Curvalicious 17
- Mini-Me 18

Chapter II: Flesh, Melanin & Eyewater
- The 1st Time a Girl Dies 20
- A Daughter's Mother 21
- Reconciliation Procrastination 22
- Disappointment 23
- Sunday Morning 25
- Remember Me 26
- Peace in Purpose 28
- Memories before Cancer 30
- The Boy with Sickle Cell Anemia 32
- Shhh Depression 33
- Soul Dipping 34
- The Sky Cries for Me 35
- Family 36

Chapter III: Past Due Rent
- Good Sangin' 38
- Apple Pie Syndrome 39
- Country Girls 41
- Summers with Aunt Queen 42
- Mine Eyes Have Seen the Glory 43
- Political Scandal 44
- Poetic Stance 45
- The Cube 46
- 50 Years Together 47
- Future History 49
- She Ain't Me 51
- Red House with the Tin Roof 52

Chapter IV: The Introvert
- Lemon Glass 54
- Tweet 55
- Office Attire 56
- Drama Leeches 58
- Mind Your Own Business 59

    Silence 60
    Evolution of a Name 61
    Child of a Teenage Mother 62
    The Stormy Drive 64
    Glory Road 65

Chapter V: Oiled Wings
    I Have a Man 68
    The Movement 69
    Income Tax Child 71
    Wasted Breath 72
    Hey Kid, You're Screwed 73
    Saturday Night (Young Mothers) 75
    The Break Up 76
    Micro Poem #3 77
    Stankin' 78
    Game Recognizes Game 80
    Relationships Ain't for Everybody 81
    Love's Heartbreak 82

Chapter VI: Emotional
    Poetry is My Boyfriend 86
    Cool Drink 88
    Battered Woman 89
    Micro Poem #1 90
    Winter Spooning Weather 91
    Cougar 92
    Up All Night 93
    Men with Sexy Hair 94
    What a Woman Wants 95
    Confessions of a Woman Scorned 96

Chapter VII: Sharp Edges, Smooth Curves
    Just Do It 98
    Boys to Men 99
    Love Jones (In the Morning) 100
    Come Away with Me 102
    Love's Strength 104
    Write About You 105
    Spring Love 106
    Autumn Days 107
    Micro Poem #2 108
    Love, Lies & Lunacy 109
    Flow Harder 110

About the Author 112

Introduction

Writing my first collection of poetry, Beautiful Conscious Love, was such a positive learning experience. If you really want to know what you're made of write and publish a book of poetry! I dealt with pain I thought was gone, memories I thought were buried and the kind of love that I wish happened more often. No, the poems aren't all autobiographical, but they are all personal. While writing this book I realized there's a reservoir somewhere deep inside my heart that has been storing all my feelings over the years. To continue to grow as a writer I've had to learn to tap into those feelings. As a self-proclaimed nerd I never relied heavily on feelings, just my intellect. That's probably the reason why I had no interest in poetry until I was in my late 20s. I had already graduated from college before I read anything by Maya Angelou and Nikki Giovanni. I didn't grow up knowing any eccentric or socially conscious people who read Langston Hughes and studied Black history. In high school my poems began with "roses are red and violets are blue". I was a simple country girl who thought the whole world ate sweetened rice for breakfast like I did. I think my dreams were small because at that time my world was small. But I'm convinced that every creative aspect of my life, every dark day, and every happy minute was a part of God's bigger plan for me.

Poetry has taught me to embrace my moments, nurture my gifts and require nothing but the best from myself. I have performed my poems dozens of times in front of hundreds of people. My creativity has manifested itself in numerous ways and I'm thankful for every blessing I've been given. Now that the book is complete and I sit here thinking about what I want to do next, I'm beginning to accept the fact that I am a *writer, a poet* and an *artist*.

I've come a long way since performing at my first open mic. I was nervous and my mouth felt like it was full of cotton balls. I didn't invite anyone to come listen to me that night just in case I chickened out at the last minute. But ultimately, that night was meant to be. When it was my turn to read I didn't make eye contact with the crowd. I read my poem about my brother's tragic and untimely death like it was etched in my brain. I expressed feelings that I had never shared with anyone. For just a few minutes I felt free from the anxiety of holding all that pain inside. And like bait dangling from a fishing pole during a hot Alabama summer, I was hooked.

Writing this book gave me with that same feeling of freedom all over again. I conjured up memories then I set them free. My desire is that everyone who reads this book feels that same sense of freedom through my words. I hope you feel free to think or rethink, free to mourn or dream, free to love or let go, free to laugh or cry, free to change or stay the same.

In the end, my purpose is to inspire. With open arms I invite you to walk into my heart and explore all that is there. Walk in, not as strangers but as friends, and experience Beautiful Conscious Love.

~Kimeko Farrar

Chapter I

BEAUTIFIED

"Someone can plant the seed of negativity around you but you don't have to water it." ~ChUC

BADD Chick

This chick is BADD and don't even know it
Just because she has the body of a dancer
She feels like she needs to show it
For that attention she be craving
Cutting up and misbehaving
Trying to make someone love her
Trying to fill a void and feel loved
She takes on a lover
Without understanding that her body is not for play
Or sold for pay
Every time she gives of herself
Or down plays her worth
She's giving the most important parts of herself away
Hoping for something in return
Something that will soothe that burn in her chest
And the scar she inherited, not earned
A broken spirit is a sucker for attention
She's falling into statistics
Maybe 'cause Mama didn't know
Or Daddy didn't show
Or someone with some sense didn't mention
That's she's a BADD chick
BADD and more than the smile on her face
BADDer than the size of her lips
Or the fullness of her hips
BADDer than the clothes she wears
Or how she styles her hair
She's a BADD girl
With all those dreams sitting in her head
BADDer than how she performs in the bed
BADD with all that talent in your voice and your dance
BADD enough to have doctor's hands
You BADD girl
Really BADD
Stop looking for other people to validate you
If no one ever believes in you
You believe in you
If no one ever claps for you
You clap for you

There's no past that can hold you in a box
That's too small for you if you don't want it to
Your thoughts are the only thing controlling you
Break through walls that you've taped your dreams to
Before those vivid pictures fade into despair and abuse
Carry yourself like there's greatness inside of you
'Cause you're a BADD chick
Just in case no one has ever told you

Black Girls Rock

I am a woman
Woman, I am
Soft and sweet
But tough as sand eroding underneath
To form rock
Hard, tested, unbreakable rock
Like Black girls rock
We girls rock and roll and pump our fists
We write, compose and produce hits
We rock math, science and medicine
Whether we're tan challenged
Or heavy on the melanin
See, I am a woman
Woman, I am
We girls rock business suits, afros and stilettos
We rock the babies, the vote and we rock the boat
If I wear my hair long with curls
Or gloss my lips
If I appear camera ready
And stick out my hips
I can love, give energy and change the world
For every man, woman, boy and girl
See, I am a woman
Woman, I am
We girls are southern slang
East coast swag
And Midwest smooth
We're those notes that make the groove hot
We're that extra pigment that makes vibrant colors pop
Yes, girls, we rock
What if I don't care about
A tight butt
Toned thighs
Or the fine lines around my eyes
What if I'm okay with letting gravity have its way
What if my walk ain't sexy

And my laugh ain't cute
What if I prefer flats over high heel boots
Still I am a woman
Woman, I am
See, I rock because I'm a
Mother
Friend
Daughter
Teacher
Fierce
Engineer
Homemaker
Preacher
Intellectual
Spiritual
Sometimes emotional
Does that make me less special
Less powerful
Less beautiful
Am I less flesh
Less blood
Less brain
Less womb
Am I less of a woman because you don't rock to my tune
Baby, I make nations bow down when I enter a room
I'm more complex than a physics exam
Read 2nd Samuels
And ask David what effect I can have on a man
I am a woman
Woman, I am

Look at Me

In motion
The span of my hips
The curve of my thighs
The arch of my back
The flesh of my calves
Evoke emotion
He notices
Eyes of sparkling espresso
Heart-shaped lips and midnight-blue curls
A bended wrist upon my chin
A mind in contemplation
Visually infatuated
He listens
To the whisper of my giggle
The sweetness of my cry
The intensity of my moan
The octave of my song
Time is borrowed from reality
Roles are played
Be a freak in the bed but a lady in the street
Cook and clean and only be seen
Never whine, complain, nag, or ask for anything
I'm superwoman without appearing to be
Waiting on the prize I exhaust myself
I reach out to him for help, out of character
I ask for his words of comfort with modest expectation
I forget something important, he is bothered by it
I de-cape to be regular and vulnerable
But he says I've changed
Truths are revealed
Perfection estranged
The pedestal on which I'm perched is cracked and leaning
Its strength is temporary
It cannot sustain the fullness of who I really am
Aspirations, hesitations, and trepidations spill over
They expose themselves
I was perfectly made and beautifully flawed when we met
I didn't pray for him to save me but to know me deeply
And he would have
If he had done more than just look at me

Make Me Over

I'm picky
Give me
Those eyes
That hair
Those thighs
Make me over – make me up
Make me look like a star
Take everything I have and make it better
Make me a little bit better than you are
If I'm gonna shop I want the best
Toned biceps
DD breasts
And a tight ass
Jenny Craig
Weight Watchers
Nutrisystem
I beg you
Make me pretty
While you make me healthy
I can have the world if I'm skinny, right
There are no unhappy people in the commercials
There are no unhappy people in my circle
Please oh please
Gimme skinny knees
And a slimmer waist
I don't have time to waste
I'm not looking for a husband
But I'm waiting for him to find me
He needs to have a stable career
Nice abs
Straight teeth, mostly his
Loves to talk
Good with kids
Doesn't play video games

Classic good looks
Christian
Loves to have fun
Doesn't own guns
Understanding and supportive
Has all his hair and his own place
Never been married
Financially secure
So I have to look good, right
To attract mister do right
Wait, wait, did I hear you right
You're going to suck the fat from where
Put a tube where
Cut what from where
Let me rethink this
I suddenly feel like I don't care

Naturalista

She stares in the mirror
Trying to look past what others think of her
Her eyes must be trained to see her new beauty
The deep down to the bone kind
Outside opinions matter less than her own
The only admiration needed is from herself
She examines the shape of her head
Wonders if those little rolls on her nape
Are an indication of her curl pattern coming in
With so little hair she finally sees her face
Because that's all that's there
Queenly images emerge in her mind
Locs, coils, curls, and knots
Kinks, buns, twists, and puffs
She feels a newness trickle down her spine
Like warm water on sore muscles
She has tapped into an awesome awareness
And breathes in the goodness she feels she's doing for herself
She cloaks herself in sunshine's fabric
A yellowish-green printed skirt and a fitted tangerine shirt
Big ceramic earrings with painted on lions hang from her ears
She knows she's fierce
As fierce and as brave as a lion for going against the grain with her mane
A grain embedded so deeply into the psyche
It's become an eternal stain on the brain
She stands up against stares, snickers and sneers
And comments from family, friends and strangers
"What did you do to your head?"
"The natural thing ain't for everybody"
Meaning
That ain't cute on you, and if you ain't cute, you ain't much
She knows there's some societal truth to that
She knows it ain't for everybody

But neither is
Money and power
Success and fame
Or children and marriage
Because everybody can't handle it
They ain't built for it
Just ain't equipped for it
But nobody can say it ain't for her
But her

Social Media

For those of you who don't know me
Wondering who I'm supposed to be
I am that chick
With thoughts so thick
Like cold syrup
From aunt jemima
Blessed with good sense
And country grammar
When I speak this
There's no pretense
I know who I be
I be she
That's country
Grew up on rural route 2
Before they named the streets

I'm just trying to put a smile on your face
Put you into your emotional good place
Better jump on it if you want it
You know it
I'm not a rapper
I'm a poet

I have a presence
Presence of mind and a little word play to go with it
So now that you know who I am
Y'all we fam
When you see me
Hold up your phones and take a pic
Send it to Facebook, Twitter and Instagram
And hashtag
Y'all need to know this chick

Shoe Game

There's actually something that's stranger than fiction
Something that can potentially drag you down
Drag you down quicker than being tied to the back of the Loch Ness Monster
It's an addiction
Unlike a sentence that's handed to you after a murder conviction
Addiction makes you map out your own self-imposed restrictions
You vow not to take that next hit
Or at least not to hit it too hard
You walk away from your Visa card
Like church after the benediction
You wanna get your stuff in order
You're on a mission
But life keeps resurfacing your hidden afflictions
So like a confident peacock with new feathers
Whether to shine or be still is a constant decision
Everyday feels like a 24-hour AA meeting
Your head plays the same greeting
To the utility company
The phone company
And your past due magazine subscriptions
Umm, hi, my name is…
Insert your name here
I've fallen a little behind this year
Yeah, I know I'm the only one to blame
I promise I'll send you a lil something next month
Summer is coming
I'm working on my shoe game

Black Doll

Little girls want to be protected
Nurtured and accepted
For whatever they are
Whoever they are
Despite skin tone or hair type
Sometimes this one thing
Isn't comprehended so easily
Sometimes little girls need a push
A nudge
A pat
To get them on the right mental track
Of self-acceptance
Or self-awareness
And understanding that black is neither worse nor better
But still beautiful
Comes when others acknowledge it for no reason at all
You don't have to remind a pretty girl that she's black
No more than you have to tell a tall girl that she's tall

Growing up my blackness was connected to circumstances
Like having a black mama and daddy with a wide nose
And a black grandmother who still worked in the cotton fields
Like putting pieces of broomsticks in my ear piercings
So the holes wouldn't close
Or living in a neighborhood where poor white folks
And poor black folks stayed on opposite sides of the road
I couldn't get any blacker if I tried

But when a white girl from school asked me to her slumber party
I cried, cried, and cried
And cried some more
Until Mama said I could go
I was scared
Back then I was always told

That white folks didn't like black folks
And black folks couldn't trust white folks
It's a message that constantly twirled around in my head
So when Mama pulled the Trans Am into their driveway
I immediately felt like I didn't want to stay
Before I could turn and tell Mama so
Everyone came running out the door and rushed me inside
So I told Mama bye

We ate cake and ice cream
We played games and danced around in our pajamas
Then we opened gifts
First, the birthday girl
Then us too
Yes, all the guests got gifts
I knew that was something that poor black folks didn't do
We each got a brand new Barbie doll
But mine was different
She had long black hair
Good hair
And fancy clothes
Red lips and a skinny nose
And her skin was dark
She was beautiful

That was the start of barriers being broken
And negative images being torn apart
I'm sure my friend's mother didn't think much of it
She thought she was given me what I was used to
I doubt they knew
I had received my first black doll that day
After that
I never saw my blackness in quite the same way

First Lady

A perfect picture of poise and grace
A mixture of extraordinary courage
Sister girl attitude
And sense of style
Her image will linger in the minds of my generation
And generations to come
Catering to those of us in need of something positive to look up to

Girls and Pigtails
-for the Duckworths

Wake up, child
I know it's early
But it's time to start the Saturday morning routine
Time to make that bushy hair sleek and clean
We need to get those ends in good condition
Before our Sunday morning tradition
That's just how the weekends go
Twist and cornrow so those strands will grow
Pretty them up with intricate parts and luscious curls
Everything is a reflection of how much I love you
There's so much joy in having little girls

Curvalicious
-for Marquita and Terasha

They say to have a waist this small
And hips this wide
Makes most men goo-goo eyed
They say that a body stacked like that
Must be cornbread and fried chicken fed
Work that thang girl
Go 'head

I say a black girl's curves defy explanation
Or calculation
No amount of calorie manipulation
Or red velvet cake
Can produce the figure eights we make
Unless it's just in your genes

Mini-Me
-for Haley

The same eyes
The same nose
The same mannerisms
One day I looked up and your face was my face
My goodness, how time flies
I wish I could've frozen you in white hard-bottom shoes
I wish I could've stopped time
Back when you first tried to walk in my high heels
Now your feet are bigger than mine
Biology is no match for time
Because time really flies
My goodness, how time flies
You're a young lady now
I'm scared to think about letting you go out into the world
Into the badness, the greatness, the pain
And into the happiness of the world
It's hard for me to let you go through life
Without being tainted
By my experiences and what I've seen
But I must let you fly
Laugh, cry and experience your own things
I'm sure this is just the beginning
Of the amazement I'll see
As you blossom naturally over time
From a princess into a queen
My goodness, how time flies

Chapter II

FLESH, MELANIN & EYEWATER

"Change is inevitable. Liking it is optional." ~ChUC

The 1st Time a Girl Dies

Her young eyes have seen disgusting death
And she's died more than once
On Friday nights
And even Wednesday afternoons during summer vacation
She's seen the ugly face and the naked torso of death
More than she's seen maple leaves turn red and back green again
But nothing is like the first time
Its interest convinced her she was special
And taught her how to swap apple-flavored Jolly Ranchers while kissing
Each time dying a sweet death
Stealing life from her until there was nothing left
No innocence
Just the sweetness between her thighs
And the chinkiness of her eyes
That brought the boys and sometimes the grown men by
Death has sucked on her neck and locked her in rooms
Called her names
Pretended she was the blame
He says nobody will believe her
She thinks it's true
'Cause nobody sees this death but her
Nobody recognizes this death but her
Not the first, second or even the third time
They just keep letting her die because they're blind
And she dies and dies and dies
On the inside
Until the scent between her thighs becomes too womanly
And death unleashes its grasp
Then she's left to live
In silence
Because silence is all that's left

A Daughter's Mother
-for Brooklyn & Keanna

Her tiny hands and feet
Have formed with awesome wonder
She is precisely perfect
You have nurtured her internally
Though you know not the color of her eyes
Or the curve of her brow
You have accumulated enough love for her
To last a lifetime
You will strength into her bones
Fight into her spirit
And love into her heart
Why?
Because you are her mother

Reconciliation Procrastination
Originally Published in *Oil & Water… and Other Things that Don't Mix* Anthology

On a Sunday afternoon drive
I lose myself in remembering, and then hours pass
Memory Lane dead ends in front of home but I can't see it
Because this house is in the way
It's worn and tattered with falling shutters and chipped paint
Faint traces of the pristine whites and yellows of my childhood remain
No roses, irises, or sunflowers though
No plum trees, no strawberry patches, no garden of collards
Bald spots in the grass indicate neglect
No man around I suppose
Children look in my direction but none rush to say hello
They don't know me
"You kids live here?"
My Alabama twang comes back
They nod their heads and I assume we're related
They fight each other over the porch swing
There, a sweet old lady used to smoke Viceroy 100s
The paper says she went on to glory a few days ago
I stand at the door and bat away old hurts
I knock because it's time
Fractures of our lives don't mend like broken bones
I say a prayer and hope that returning home is a splint

Disappointment

Disappointment can swell in your chest like the wind at the eye of a hurricane
It tastes bitter
Like a red apple that bloomed in winter
Disappointment tugs at your self-esteem and leaves you feeling empty inside
It makes you question every dream you've had
Doubt every answer you thought was right
And reconsider everything you know to be wrong

Disappointment snatches credibility from your faith
It raises up old heartaches you spent so much time burying
It makes you believe you are unworthy

Disappointment is like an old mista
It doesn't creep up on you real soft and talk sweet to you
It hollers at you
Calls you out your name
Makes you ashamed of being you

Oh but disappointment doesn't stop at shame
It makes you regret, too
Regret that you even stood tall, branched out or woke up
When disappointment gets hold of you
When you let it get in your blood and mix with your DNA
It has no mercy
It doesn't care about anything you've accomplished before
Doesn't care about your soul
Or the music that used to play in your heart
It bangs at your chest with the force of an ocean's tide
Like your heart is no longer there
And for a moment you ain't living
And you ain't existing
Even though you're still breathing

Disappointment is stingy, lazy, crazy, and selfish
It prefers to have you to himself
And each time you give in to disappointment
It gets bigger and bigger until you break under its weight
Then, it feeds on your broken-ness
Until your spirit lies helpless among the shattered pieces of your life

And you have nothing left to give
But strong are those who pull hope and victory from nothing
And snatch joy from the jaws of disappointment
Again, and again, and again
Because if you're ever going to be anything and make it in this life
You can never let disappointment win

Sunday Morning

Lift me up a little higher
So I can see over the Monday morning blues that are already starting to set in
And I can move beyond the mistakes I made last week

Heal whatever problems are testing my faith
In my body, my mind, my spirit
Because I desire
To have the physical strength to handle whatever obstacles are sent to make me stronger
I desire
To have enough wisdom to make decisions untainted by present circumstances or worldly desires
I desire
To be filled with enough patience and peace to wait on what is meant for me

Lift me up a little higher
Not so I can rise above others
And not so I can be more than I need to be
But so I can pull as many as possible up with me
And they can benefit from the journey I have been promised
I want to have your favor
Because I shied away from greed, selfishness and pettiness
I give all I have with every heave of my chest and bat of my eyelash
I will not get tired, I will not give up, I will not give out
So in the end
I can be lifted up a little higher

Beautiful Conscious Love

Remember Me
-For South Haven Elementary

If there is ever a senseless tragedy that happens to me
If you never did anything to raise the awareness before it happened in our community
Then please by all means
After-the-fact
Pray
But don't just pray for me
Instead
Move for me
Take a stand for me
Fight for a change
So my pain isn't in vain as you mourn for me
Increase the love so high
That this dirt and these clouds can't block it from me
Love is the key
It unlocks doors, hearts and minds
It's the only thing that's gonna cut down on these tragedies
That's removing precious lives from their families
When I'm gone I know you'll be missing me
I'm trying to send you some positive energy
So you can stand bold
A tree is no stronger than the roots it grows
And no more important than the fruit it holds
Those fruits of memories
So I need you to dig deep
Branch out in the midst of craziness
I want you to pray hard without ceasing
But you can't just pray for me
Be an advocate for healing and the understanding
Of the mentally disturbed
The socially perturbed
And the pain stricken suburbs
Without confrontation evil can win so easily
So like a stick of butter on a hot smoking stove
Spread the word of peace
And love until love tops the mountains and floods the seas
Sometimes when things happen
There is a bigger meaning that can heal our sorrow

If we truly believe
There's work to be done in the world
And our own footprints or lack thereof
Are like breadcrumbs tracing back to our humanity
The prayers we pray are directly proportional to how far in love we've journeyed
Sometimes the road is long
Sometimes the road is steep
Sometimes the road is scary
But it allows every man, woman, boy, and girl
To finally be seen for the love they need
I beg of you to stay on the road
So I don't have to welcome another soul to glory too early
If I ever leave this place in a tragic and untimely way
Do this in remembrance of me

Peace in Purpose

Peace
Peace doesn't come with laws, rules and war
Peace comes from standing on your feet and chasing the truth you seek
Peace comes from understanding your purpose
And knowing that in the thick of discomfort and defeat
God's favor rests with us
No doubt with the richest of the rich
But especially with the rest of us
Just like Mary
Who gave birth to the son of God behind stable doors
We are all his people
God promised to send a Messiah
One who would take us higher
One who could save every man, woman, boy, and girl
So he sent Jesus
Under the humblest of circumstances to a corrupted world
And even though it's only mandated that his death be celebrated
In his birth we find joy
Who cares that we can't pinpoint the exact day of his birthday
It's merely a symbol of when the angels appeared before shepherds
To tell them where Jesus lay
And a bright star in the sky signaled the birth of a new king
And the wisest of men walked miles to bring
Gifts of gold, frankincense and myrrh to welcome him
But back then
Kinda the same way as today
People can treat your good news like it's the blues
'Cause they're longing to walk in your shoes
Again
This is where understanding your purpose
And peace in knowing comes in
You best believe that if you are anointed and chosen
Haters are out to do you in
King Herod was afraid that Jesus was meant to take his crown
'Cause he was born near his town
And he wasn't about to let that go down
So Herod committed one of the earliest tragedies against humanity
Before amber alerts and gun violence documentaries

To take out Jesus,
He ordered every child to be killed who was under the age of two
But Mary and Joseph got a warning
And fled with Jesus to Egypt
See when God is for you nobody can be against you
There was a perfect plan for Jesus
And there's one for me and you, too
So during these trying times
When troubles are all around
And the world seems to be spinning backwards
And turning upside down
Just remember the spiritual star that was used as a guiding light
And reflect on how Jesus was sent as a comforter to show us
What real love feels like

Memories before Cancer

She used to be somebody's dream
Somebody's baby
Before I knew her
And before I was my mother's child
She used to play in fields of high weeds and red clay
And she hoped to finish the sixth grade
She was poor and later she was orphaned
But still, she saw the world fondly
Past women's emancipation, segregation and finally integration
My grandmama

She used to be a drinker, a smoker, a party-er, and a little bit nosey too
Before she got saved that is
She used to curl her hair with strips of brown paper sacks
And scent herself with oils
She wore bold print dresses
And painted her fingernails red to match her lips
Causing men to swarm around our front porch like bees
I observed of course
She was my grandmama

She used to be my caregiver, my cook, and my companion
Because every morning I woke up, she was there
She used to buy me penny candy and Pepsi every first of the month
Because I asked her to
When Mama would try to make me do housework
She would say, "That girl don't know nothing 'bout washing no dishes. Gone somewhere and play, child"
Grandmama got it
And if my memory serves me correctly, she used to have jet black hair
She used to have skin that was firm and smooth and joints that were agile
Until it happened
And when it happened
It knocked me to my knees like I was the one who had it
I used to have a brother that I buried four months earlier
So selfishly I told the Lord I don't have any more tears to cry right now
And even though I begged and pleaded with her to hold on just a little while longer
It still diminished the youth and spirit of her I had come to know

And it left me with memories that hurt long before they brought comfort
It does not care about what used to be
It is a liar, a cheat, and a thief
It has no respect of persons
It has no respect of color, race, gender, time, love, or religion
It must be cured

The Boy with Sickle Cell Anemia

I still remember his face
I remember that he was my first crush
That was during a time when life was supposed to be simple
And you still had a lot to look forward to
When you're young
You always think you have a whole lot of time
But the only time that's guaranteed is the past

I remember that it was summer
Band camp was underway
I remember the radio blasting from my father's car
Diana Ross's "Missing You" caused tears to form in my eyes
Wasn't sure why I cried
Emotions were so new
I wasn't even a teenager yet
It was my first memorable experience of death
It was a tortured heart feeling

I remember that he was cute
Somehow that made it hurt even more
He went on to march with angels
Left his saxophone on the field that day
His cells were fighting themselves
But they're living in harmony now

I don't want to remember his pain in my tears
I just want to hear his saxophone

Shhh Depression

It's morning
Her muscles are tight and sore
The sun burns
Her teeth hurt
She wants to move
She can't move
She wants to laugh
But the TV is too loud
It's irritating
"Fake ass TV people," she mumbles to herself
She can't get comfortable
She moves from the bed to the couch
From the couch back to the bed
Stupid phone keeps ringing
Happy people keep posting Facebook statuses
She's the only one not happy
Not fulfilled
Not loved
Damn, her muscles ache like hell
Her heart hurts and she doesn't know why
Everybody's life is moving but hers
Take this pain away, she prays
Prayer isn't working
She doesn't want to see faces
Or sun
Or reminders of how she hurts so much
There's no laughter here today
Maybe tomorrow

Soul Dipping

Some souls are lost before they are born
Tortured by their own DNA
Their despair is regenerative like skin cells
Unknowingly, they rush toward their exit while running from demons
Blowing bits of themselves onto everyone they meet
As they dance, sing, speak
They are applauded with vigor
But their talents do little to buy them extra time on earth
They drown while flying
Those souls are merely disposable puppets to the masses who scream for more

More of their hollowed out insides until another puppet comes along
One who is more tormented, more damaged, more talented
Souls
Souls grow dark and tired and weary and alone
Even in rooms of massive square footage
With crystal clear windows and thousands of people
There is no hope for a tormented soul in the midst of tainted minds
But there are plenty of accolades until a greater emotional wreck emerges

The Sky Cries for Me

Isn't it funny…
How we pick and choose what we want the world to see
I'm good at it
I smile pleasantly, so no one truly
Knows how bad I feel
Isn't it foolish…
How we pretend that everything is fine and under control
When it's just make believe
Every turn I make takes me farther away
And I struggle through some days
Isn't it crazy…
How you'll never know if I need a strong shoulder or helping hand
Because I keep it to myself
That's just who I am
I won't tell my closet friend
Isn't it silly…
How I have to be strong, I can't be weak, and I won't break down
Then you assume
That my silence means I'm okay
So you don't call to see about me today
When I can't hide my fears - no more
And my eyes won't privately shed their tears - no more
Just in time, before I'm exposed and uncovered
Showers of rain begin to fall down all around me
The wind screams, the thunder roars, and the sky cries for me.

Family

An old woman stands in the center of the room
In the center of family
She looks into their faces
She sees love, pain, laughter, pride, and memories
They have her struggles, her joys, her blood running through their veins
Like water from a free flowing stream
In their faces she sees everything
All her dreams
Her dreams that someday their family name will mean
That nothing she did in her small fragile life was in vain
Family will pick up the torch where she left it
And carry it to higher heights
They will spring up from defeat every time they get knocked down with it
And pass it on when they're gone
Because family is about that link between one another
How we're connected to one another
Having a love that can't be broken
Even when trust is broken
Because you have that chain that genetically connects you
Connects what I'm going through to what you're going through
Nurture that bond so petty things don't separate you
Rejoice in the bloodlines that have defined so much of you

Chapter III

PAST DUE RENT

"Your attitude towards problems will determine if you wake up in the morning without any." ~ChUC

Good Sangin'

C'mon sista!
Throw your head back
Lift up your manicured hand
Point your finger like you're talking to me
Fill your lungs full of air
Open your mouth wide
Wail
Praise
Testify
Make the rafters vibrate
Make the pews sweat
Make Mother Burkes run the aisles
I need to feel something
I know a blessing for me is on the tip of your tongue
I need you to do your good sangin' this morning

Apple Pie Syndrome

The world is suffering from a sickness that causes cerebral dysfunction
It's where the connection between the heart and the mind malfunctions
I'm not mentally ill but my ills are mental
And whether you take 285 through Atlanta
Or the red line to Harlem is inconsequential
'Cause we're all just partially free in a society that's still experimental
The socially retarded has us boxed into a system that's departmental
Where hopes, dreams and goals are bought and sold
Like thirty-day storage rentals
And large corporations write job offers in pencil
And politicians no longer focus on the poor
But the middle class with more voting potential
Serving up apple pie rhetoric and praising education's credentials
Expecting the seeds of torn down generations
To understand that reading is fundamental
When they can't get enough role models in their hood to act parental or influential
34% of our own children live in poverty
That number should make you tremble
But instead of starving poverty like the fever
We keep feeding our sickness with apple pie

We all want our piece of the pie
The white picket fence
The house on the hill with umpteen bedrooms and gazillion bathrooms
So everybody can piss at the exact same time if they want too
We want 10 figure incomes
$100,000 cars
And 2.5 kids with good hair
All these dreams are as American as apple pie
But somewhere a broken-hearted mother from Somalia
Left her starving and dehydrated kid on the side of a dusty road to die as they fled from famine
While here
We stuff our faces full of apple pie
The poor in London riot
'Cause they're tired of seeing fortune dangled in their faces
And they have absolutely no way of grabbing it
But here
Money hungry executives haven't outsourced our educated

And highly skilled jobs to China yet
So we continue to eat the apple pie
Even as thousands of Ghanaian children are sold into slavery for just a few dollars
It's an image that makes me sick
But not sick enough to put my pie down

I'm torn 'cause my own life hasn't been days of nursery rhymes
And nights of milk and cookies
Life was hard - I can't lie, I want my piece of the pie
But sometimes too many apples give me indigestion
So I crave something with a little more substance
Something that will feed my spirit
But won't sit on my stomach like bowls of cornbread and buttermilk
'Cause when I'm all fat, bloated and heavy from too much apple pie
A passion for something greater than my own needs
Is the lyrical colonic that makes me spit my ass off

Spit cause some folks don't know poor
Like I know poor
Spit cause maybe you don't understand hard times
Like I understand hard times
Spit cause I'm blessed right now
But I ain't always felt highly favored
Spit cause I've been to that place where I preferred not eating
Over getting free lunch
Spit cause my grandmother had to sweep snakes from our raggedy driveway
Before I got off the school bus
Spit cause I know what it feels like to squat over an empty bucket in the wintertime
And use an outhouse in the summer
Spit cause my mama said,
"Lil girl use your head for something other than a hat rack"
I spit for starving children
Spit for worried mothers
Spit for hard working fathers
Spit because life has to be about more than getting my piece of the pie

Country Girls

Blackberry picking
Strawberry stealing
Pecan tree climbing
Muscadine finding
Creek wading
Bike riding
Pigtails flying
Old inner tube for tree swinging
Broomstick for a microphone singing
Hog slopping
Nappy hair rubber band popping
Red rover send one over
Wishing on a four-leaf clover
Run through school
This is what little country girls do

Summers with Aunt Queen

The bobbin from her pole wobbles in the water
Up and down
Up and down
But we ain't caught no fish
I spent all morning digging for worms
Putting 'em in buckets
Covering 'em with a little bit of dirt
But we ain't caught no fish
My knees are ashy
My face is molly
I smell like fishy water
But we ain't caught no fish
I always have fun though
When I'm sitting on the creek bank with Aunt Queen

Mine Eyes Have Seen the Glory

Mine eyes have seen the glory
From piss pots, slop buckets and tin roofs – no blinds
To a centrally-heated home and enough baths to pee at the same time
From a few packs of chicken thighs cooked to last seven days a week
To steamed rice, roasted red potatoes, fish only – I'll pass on the meat
Mine eyes have seen the glory
Kinky black hair, brown skin and full lips – disrespected
Sprinting for a public beach to take a dip – civil rights protected
Loving the sand between my toes and life's infinite possibilities
Years later as stretch marks, cellulite and rolls show freely
Mine eyes have seen the glory
The seeds of Negros highly educated in Calculus, sines and cosines
But morally epileptic
Seizing for prosperity
Trying to keep time
Fortune or fame is fine but neither of which do I aspire
Returning to our former virtues is my truest desire before I expire

Political Scandal

Sex, lies, money, and extortion
Fast cars and faster women
Not headlines from the latest movie reviews
But the biographies of our elected politicians
Getting a little bit on the side
Before they get down to business
Poisoned by greed and power
And easy opportunity
Misusing taxpayers' money
Has become a part of business
Securing the next election
Is the biggest part of the business
It's a shame that scandal
Is how they become household names
Maybe they are knocked senseless
By visions of Bentleys
And walking red carpets
Like the latest chart topping celebrities
Or reality TV puppets
When they get started with the deception
And dive deeper into their jaded perception of the truth
That rules are for us not them
They even have family going out on a limb
Conspiring with them or blindly looking away
To keep the fur coats and expensive gifts coming in

Poetic Stance

What are we but one person among the masses
Who long to gleam in the perfect light of love and beauty
If we were without our poetic stance

In the presence of darkness
Absent of direction
Our spirits merge with the judgment of the majority
To be accepted by the so-called acceptable

But alas, we are the newest amalgamation of our time
The technically creative and the disgustingly beautiful - poets

We should surely waste away in servitude to the green master
And the mundaneness of sustaining daily life
If not for the creativity that feeds our being with passionate dreams

Oh, those poetic dreams are sustenance to my soul
While I purposely search for a greater purpose
Between making a living

The Cube

I've lived most of my life in a cube
It's not even a full cube
It has no top
It's barely taller than I am
It's not completely stifling
It's secure
Or so I think
Even though it keeps no hatred out
And no good stuff in

Still, it's more appealing than a box
The box that sometimes holds my fears
The box that has a few cracks for air
It tries to allow my most elaborate thoughts to peak through
But only a little

My thoughts and dreams are so thirsty
If I feed them the energy they needed
They could actually grow big enough to explode the box and break free
But fears overpower dreams

I don't like the stupid box
I criticize the box like most other people do
But being disconnected from who I really am
Makes me think I'm better off in the cube
I just turn it like the Rubik's
Trying to find the perfect match
The ideal position
Ignoring the fact that I am still stuck
Inside a cube

50 Years Together

I am not ashamed
Not ashamed of my vision of fifty years in one man's arms
With love as the bond
He and I merge together into one spirit
Acting in unison
Giving God the glory for our love story
Could it be
That in this day and time of you and me
And they and them
That we could actually be a real family
Can we step away from our mothers and fathers
Our friends and foes
To run across the stars and dance on moonbeams
My mind believes that we could
My heart hopes that we will
I know it takes a special skill
To maintain a close hold on the brain
When it wants to tip toe through greener pastures
When laughter is faint
Promises are forgotten
And everybody's last name is Jones
While we can't seem to get along
They all manage to be doing much better than us
I still will not be ashamed
Because I will be yours
And you will be mine
You will be the love of my lifetime
The always in my forever
The heaven inside my earth
Even when love is broken
Our core will remain intact
God promised me that
Because I made a promise to him
Ask and you shall receive they say
So day after day
I ask and I wait
I pray that he sends me the one
Not so I can feel worthy

I've come to the conclusion that if I don't already feel that way
Then love will not work anyway
If he gives me pink
I want to give him red
If he takes me high
I want to take him higher
Together, our experiences should be intensified
I will not turn a blind eye
Nor be ashamed to speak it into existence
It's too important
To me
So I wear my heart on my sleeve
Not so he can take it as he pleases
But so when he sees it
He's more committed to taking better care of it
Because he knows that it beats for him

Future History

Some parts of our history were rough
But we can't use our past as a crutch
Or as something that handicaps us
We must use it to move us forward
Climb higher
Think bigger
Accomplish greater things
Just like there's power in the Word
There's power in words
The things we speak
The history we pass down
Is basically a testimony to show
That God doesn't put us in circumstances
And not give us the ability or opportunity to grow
Our ancestors didn't come here in ships
And survive 400 years of slavery
By being weak or meek
Everything they went through and overcame
Helped them to toughen
And because their blood is running through our veins
We have the same strength and resilience
That allowed some of our people
To be absolutely brilliant
So don't get caught up in what other people think of your dreams
If they haven't accomplished what you're trying to do
They just might try to discourage you
Some people told Madame CJ Walker that she couldn't be successful in business
But through common sense and hair care
She became the first Black millionaire
All she had to do was stay in her lane
God had already preordained her fate
See in life there are many choices we have to make
It's up to you to choose to be great
On the Underground Railroad Harriet Tubman carried a gun
She would point it at you
If a slave decided he was too tired or too scared to continue to run
She said
You can't mess up everybody else's dream or jeopardize me

So right here is where you choose to die or be free
See we all have some choices to make
When deciding what kind of people we're going to be
Whether you're young or old – you haven't peaked yet
There are options you haven't even thought of yet
Black women invented the hair brush and the keyboard stand
A black man invented the personal computer
And now they're small enough to hold in our hand
Another black man created the potato chip
And in 2008 we elected our first black president
All of this greatness is a part of our history
And we're still making things happen
In medicine, science, entertainment, sports, and politics
So keep the past in your hearts
Learn from it
Reap the benefits
'Cause through continued faith in the creator
What we do now
Could possibly be black history later

She Ain't Me

Oh, that's your new girl?
I'm happy for you
I bet you can already tell that she ain't me
That eye shadow she's wearing is cute
I almost bought the same color MAC lip gloss
But I didn't because I don't need it
I guess she does
But then again, she ain't me
Her whip is tight, mad props to her
That black leather interior is sweet
Baby, you don't have to convince me that she has money
And that her crib is banging
All that may very well be
But the fact remains, she ain't me
Wow, she has two degrees
How studious of her
My degrees raise body temps, remember?
So she can't do what I do
Because she don't know what I know
See, she ain't me.
It was good seeing you, Boo
Enjoy dinner at the fancy restaurant
What am I doing?
Nothing. I'll probably fry some chicken
Bake some yams and watch the game
Good luck to you
That's right
Turn
Walk away
And wonder why
She ain't me

Red House with a Tin Roof

I grew up in a house
There were four rooms
And a porch where we kept the coal
The firewood
And the old rocking chair
I'm pretty sure asbestos had to be there, too
Somewhere under that roof
Or in the walls
But I didn't know we were poor
The kitchen had no running water
We had a well
There was no bathroom
Just a bucket
An outhouse
And a big tin tub for bathing
But I didn't know we were poor
The living room had a big black heater
It smoked really bad
I used to find kindling to light the fire in winter
The heater had limited settings
Hot
Hella hot
Or it's so hot in here that I can't breathe hot
But I didn't know we were poor
There were two bedrooms
One for my mother and father
One for me
My brother
And my grandmother to share
But I didn't know we were poor
Back then
I didn't care

Chapter IV

THE INTROVERT

"Crying is your strength building up momentum." ~ChUC

Lemon Glass

There are memories in my lemon glass
Despite moving,
The lemon glass remains
Despite a house fire,
The lemon glass is still here
I don't care if the glass is pretty or stylish
Or if it goes with marble countertops or cherry-stained cabinets
Granny would spend her last dime for me
She'd come to my school and act a fool
Because someone stole my owl calculator
I'll cry like a baby if something ever happens to my lemon glass
It's one of the last things she gave me
Before cancer robbed her of her trips to yard sales
And the Dollar General
Before she stopped calling on check day
To make me drive her to the store
I said I wouldn't cry no more
Said I'd only fill this lemon glass with lemonade
Not tears
But sometimes I find comfort in the fact
That I still feel something after all these years

Tweet

What is this thing called
Twitter
Who does it belong to
It's Social
Really
Why do I only get 140 characters
To say profound words of wisdom
Or tightly wound nonsense
Efficiently packaged inside hashtags and at symbols
Hold on a second
I need to tweet that

Office Attire

Go 'head
Put on your black suit fresh from the cleaners
Look casket sharp
In freshly shined shoes
And black-rimmed glasses with no prescription
So you can look smarter
It's all part of the role you've been taught
It's not entirely your fault
You think you need those things to earn respect
To get ahead
Get a promotion
Even get a job that you're under-qualified for
Go 'head
Look the part
Fit in
Originality isn't for the office
It's for that place that no one cares about before 9 and after 5
Where no one takes your picture
Or knows my name
I mean your name
Where what the people there think doesn't matter
Because they don't write your review at the end of the year
After all these years
Does it matter that you're still conforming
Conforming to ideals set by a majority
Ideals that not even they all follow
But again
You've been taught that you can't do what they do
Because you have no net to catch you
They could ruin you
Before you get started
They can finish me
I mean you

The Introvert

Don't pay me no mind
Go 'head
Adjust that hair
Change your style
Don't be too threatening
Too ethnic
Too bold
Too you
Gotta let your desire for success show through
Then smile
And take what is given to you

Drama Leeches

Our society loves drama
We say we don't
But we do
We are a fickle people
Controlled by boredom and excitement
Lured by whatever looks enticing
We hate the way women are portrayed
On TV and in songs
And the way our men are degraded and belittled
Or the way the poor is ridiculed, mistreated and untrusted
But we laugh as soon as the media airs
Someone busted and disgusted on the 6:00 news
Then when it's not funny anymore
We wonder why the reporter
Picked that particular person to interview
It's a shame

Mind Your Own Business

We are all something
Liars, thieves, cheaters, sneaks,
Backstabbers, instigators, dope fiends, creeps.
My issue -- probably ain't like yours
His vice -- probably ain't like mine
But each of us deal with one
Maybe even two
This much I know is true

If I shine a spotlight on the drama
The gossiping, the fornicating and the uppity spirits
If I take special note of the neighbors'
Laziness, nastiness or cussing when I hear it
If I condemn your soul to the pits of hell
While hiding all my worldly sins
Then I should bite my tongue with all my teeth
Before I speak
To quote Matthew, Mark or 2nd Corinthians.

A bird cannot fly with the weight of a thousand wings
No more than a man is perfect at everything
You can buy my faults for a hundred dimes
Go ahead -- analyze them -- see what you find
But focusing on everybody's wrongs is never right
It's just a waste of valuable time…

Silence

Alone in my room
I hear the dryer
The drum turns
My shirt buttons scrape the sides
I'm extremely tuned into the sound
I have nothing else to do
Nothing to do except reflect and wonder
On how I got here
Alone in my room
Again

Evolution of a Name

My name is Kimeko
That's what it says on my birth certificate
When I was born
I was nicknamed Kim
A variation of the real thing
Later I was called "rip it up"
Then I was Fatty
And then I was called Meko
Another variation
I've been called
Baby
Sweetheart
Boo
And babe
But to be honest
I really prefer Kimeko

Child of a Teenage Mother

My hands tell the story of my life
Lotions and moisturizers
Can't smooth the wrinkles deepened by my strife
When I was just days old
Still high yella from no sun exposure
My pinky stayed wrapped around my mother's
She grew up faster than her peers
She was young
Just sixteen years older than me
Fifteen if you count when I was conceived

I've been told that once she laid me down to sleep
I twisted and turned until I fell from the sheets
Nobody thought to look for me
But there I was
Beneath the bed
Sound asleep
Hands tucked under my head
I had to be tough
I was the child of a teenage mother

At the age of thirteen, I learned that life was real
My hands hardened and callused from working in cotton fields
I jumped out of bed at 5 am and chose my first row
Mista Charlie looked in my direction
And said I was good with a hoe
I hated the ignorance oozing from his words
But that was something I dared not say
I knew if I did as my Granny did
Mista Charlie wouldn't dock my pay

So with my hoe in my hand that was much taller than me
I shook the morning dew from my pant legs
And dusted red clay from my knees
Bent over and groaning
I needed both hands to pull up the weeds
My Granny would say, "Watch your back, child, please"
I was focused
I wreaked havoc on those rows
Because I needed to buy school clothes
I learned how to work
I was the child of a teenage mother

I'm not claiming that my life was bad
I'm not claiming that all I had to endure was good either
The rain falls on the just and the unjust
There's a little bit of struggle planned for all of us
But I know that my foundation is deep
The rock on which I stand is sturdy
Not because I chose it
But because that's how it had to be
That was the plan for me
So my testimony could be given truly
To help others like me see
That you can grow beyond your wildest dreams
If someone plants that seed
I am a child of a teenage mother

The Stormy Drive

A lonely road
Sparse light
The rain descends from the night
Not in drops or drips
But in buckets
Pouring like hateful words
From a lover's lips
The smell of leather on my hands
Is embedded from a concentrated grip
The sight of one dimly lit sign ahead
Relaxes the muscles in my neck
Thank God we made it

Glory Road

My thoughts don't come in complete sentences
My poems don't come in end line rhyme
But there's a method to my madness
A vision that surpasses my own comprehension
For I could easily turn off my mind
Marry
Raise a kid
Then my biggest worry
Could be how pretty I'm going to be tomorrow
But that vision fills me with emptiness
No matter how many times I try to make sense of it
I just get nothing from it
So I keep pounding the pavement on this hard road
Comparing myself to my heroes
She-roes
Trying not to be buried a zero
And stuck in the middle of complacency
With dreams sealed up in my coffin
There's nowhere for my soul to go
Unless I stay on this glory road

Chapter V

OILED WINGS

"If bad things keep happening to you, you're probably missing the lesson."
~ChUC

I Have a Man

I have a man
A tall good-looking brother
Size 12 shoe
Relaxed jeans
Polo shirt wearing brother
I have a man
He works hard
And plays hard
He calls me to check in throughout the day
He's always on the go
Making moves
His friends can't do without him
He's focused on his vision
Wish I knew where I fit in
Doesn't matter though
'Cause I have a man
He's out
I'm home
But he'll text me before long
To check in again
I'm kinda feeling like my home
Is a 24-hour 7-Eleven
Always open like IHOP
Waiting for him to get a few minutes to stop
And drop by
Never on the first class ride
Always on stand by
Even though I have a man

The Movement

I heard a voice saying there should be a movement
There will be a movement
He will lead the movement
Even though I didn't know him
I've never met him
I felt his pain just the same
So I knew the voice had to be true
I felt the fear of the first bang ripping through the air
Felt legs too stunned to run
And a dry mouth filled with screams
I smelled the stench of blood mixed with sweat-soaked hair
And I remembered a hate I thought I had reconciled
I didn't know him
I've never met him
But I felt his pain just the same
I heard harsh words and hearts beating fast
Heard the thumping sounds of bodies against fists
I felt the pebbles of the concrete as he fell
Felt the stillness of his body lying there
Felt precious life ooze into the wind, leaving a lesson to be used
I felt the heaviness of the air because his soul was floating on the molecules
And as his case grew cold I felt the broken heart that only a grieving mama knows
See, there should be a movement
There will be a movement
I know it wasn't his plan, but he will lead the movement
I didn't know him
I've never met him
But I felt his pain just the same
I heard the screams of that mama so vividly
That the pain in my stomach felt like my ovaries had ruptured
And my fallopian tubes tied themselves
'Cause there's no way in hell I'll ever birth another seed
Into this land of big gun toting egos and greed

That makes me doubt I'll ever have a son
Snatching the football out of his hand before he's tossed one
Stealing my hopes of his Master's degree before he can count to one
Got me all balled up and crying for a mama who has lost her youngest one
I mean really, there should be a movement
One that calls for truth and justice and understanding
For when the people are moved something special should follow
Now my heart breaks 'cause he's the one who had to lead the movement
But without it there will only be silent outrage, howling cries into the night
And frustrated whispers of
Will my baby be next
If the movement doesn't come
See, we didn't know him
We've never meet him
But we felt his pain just the same
And something within us stirs and moves
Because we could all be him

Income Tax Child

Rim shops get ready
The economy is about to get a boost
I'll let you claim mine for 1200
Mama's gotta get paid, too
The car payment's 30 days late
Can't save nothing
The refund is already spent
I'm depending on my dependant
To get me caught up on my past due rent

Wasted Breath

She asked me what I thought, and I told her everything
Everything I had read and heard and seen and gone through myself
And I told her with a smile
With no hate, envy or ulterior motives
Just love
Being careful to think only of her and not myself
With each word I spoke, she nodded in agreement
She even said an amen or two
But I knew

I knew as she fidgeted with her hair that her mind had left the room
I wasn't really speaking the words she wanted to hear
But I never did
You don't milk a cow expecting to drink juice, do you?
But still
She would ask and I would give
Even as she began to dream up another plan
One more feasible to her
A plan very different from the one we discussed
One that would not meet my approval of course
Because it was rooted in fantasy, not reality

I saw what she could not see
But I could not force my hand with my friend
In the end
I hugged her, said goodbye and wished her the best
I felt the déjà vu of the conversation
I knew we would be having it again, soon
Since she had not listened or learned anything
Since the last blue moon

Hey Kid, You're Screwed

I was engrossed in a daydream
In this dream
I was in a deep conversation with my 14-year-old self
I was trying to tell this 14-year-old girl about love
She wasn't trying to hear it
She had no interest in my eloquent speech
Unmoved by my stance on how good love feels
And how it changes the world
She said, "Love ain't all that"
Wow
Really
Just like that
Even though she was a kid from the 80s
She was obviously no 80s baby
She was tainted
And had a reality TV kind of mentality
I had to remember that this girl grew up alone
Not physically
She had plenty of people around her
But mentally
She was shut off from the world in her mind
All the bad things were just too much
Whether it was the wrong kind of love
The wrong kind of touch
Or the wrong things seen
There were places in her mind she would go
Safe places
Like memories of old sitcoms or basketball shots made
But she shied away from those dark places
Where she had to reconcile loneliness from neglect and love from abuse
So in her defense
Over time
She learned to feel nothing at all

No happiness
No sorrow
No joy
No anger
Just whatever
Whatever was better than dealing with things she had no control over
How do I get through to this girl
How do I tell her to go to the dark places and bring light
How do I finally get to finish this dream and wake up in a different world

Saturday Night (Young Mothers)

It's Saturday night
A family outing at the movies
The little boy is so excited
He can hardly keep still
This excitement will soon lead to a dreaded mistake
And seal his fate
The parking lot is filled with cars
Big, small, expensive, and hoopties
He weaves his body between them
Jumping and bouncing with his arms flailing
He bumps one
The car alarm starts wailing
It makes us all jump
We burst into laughter like normal college students
The boy's mother looks toward us
She is not amused
She pays no attention to our faces
That show we could care less about her son
Or the alarm
It isn't our car
She's embarrassed by his unruliness
That's really only perceived by her
She can't rationalize that those new car alarm systems are sensitive
They go off when the wind blows
The poor kid braces for what he already knows is coming
She lunges at him
Screams a few cuss words
Before smacking him clean across his face
We stand there
We're in shock
He's not
Young mothers

The Break Up

My heart is heavy and I can't shake it
Guess I'll have to fake it 'til I can make it
When you give your heart there's a chance someone will break it
So if love decides to beat you up and kick you down
All you can do is take it

Greatness was impregnated in me so I birthed it
I will give him two months to see it wasn't worth it
Accepted my heart then like Pee-Wee Herman in a movie theater
He jerked it
School is out
The bell has rung
In case you haven't heard it
Eyes up pencils down
The lesson is done
Check the blackboard for your next assignment son
Cause I just dismissed the room with this one

Micro Poem #3

Pain
Just like rain
Doesn't have to fall hard
To affect everything it touches

Stankin'

Something stanks
It's foul
Like I burned the grits while taking a shower again
Air freshener just lies on top of the scent
Makes it smell like sweet stank
Much like nasty attitudes and smiling faces
Nasty stank on the inside
Sweet air freshener on the outside
Someone needs to invent a stank detector
Let it wail
Scream
And holla
Before stank consumes me
Chokes me
And surrounds my body like the smoke from 1000 cigars
Maybe we can place the stank detector in clubs
And at work
Or even in churches and schools
'Cause when stank gets in your spirit
It's hard to get out
And stank seems to congregate in places we frequent the most
Places full of good people
In the places where you think people are for you
But they really ain't thinking about you
Not in a positive way
In places where you're supposed to find a good man or a good woman
But they really only flash those air freshener smiles that look good in public
Beware
Those smiles have a 30-day stank blocker
Plenty enough time for you to get caught up in the fake pheromones
And fall in love
Charge up your credit card
Start thinking about having his babies
Scaling down your dreams

But building up his
Trying to fix things about yourself that don't need to be fixed
Cooking things you don't eat
Saying you like sitting on the couch all day
When you really like going out
Hiding your money so he doesn't feel bad about not having any
Feeding his insecurities and calling it compromise
And giving too much of yourself
All to your demise
Before you take a 30ML dose of the truth
That opens up your nostrils like Theraflu
Before your nose starts to get
Itchy
Irritated
Immune to the air freshener
And like old gym shoes left in a closed bag for months
Something is stankin'
You realize it's your new boo

Game Recognizes Game

I saw your eyes wandering
Glazed over in admiration
Checking out the chick's curves
And her cute face
Pondering what you'd like to do
If I weren't sitting in plain view
I noticed her
So I expected you to notice her, too
I'm no fool
I know what the beauty of a woman can do
I'm guilty maybe
Of using my female power occasionally
So it's not that I'm mad that you looked
Or stared intently at her as she walked in the room
I'm not mad that you admired her body, face or style
It's just that I haven't seen you look at me like that in a while
That's why I'm pissed

Relationships Ain't for Everybody

I'm better off free
I'm a runner
Always have been
Always will be
Being able to distance myself from the world
Separate myself from the wind
Has been my refuge
My retreat

Maybe I let you hold on to me too tightly
Let you kiss me too lightly
And I slipped into unfamiliar territory
How did I get to this place?
Here
Where I can't see my face for your face
Can't tell your voice from mine
I'm not sure I like this oneness
It's kinda suffocating
Can't even cough and clear my throat
You're in the way
Is that what a relationship is supposed to be?
No more you
No more me
Just an indefinite compromise
So we can be us
You're cute
But I'm kinda missing who I was before

Love's Heartbreak

It's dawn
I haven't slept much
I'm still thinking of his touch
Thoughts of him keep creeping into my mind
His smell keeps sweeping past my nose
His voice is like a constant ringing in my ear
I pray for this pain to be over
Days start to feel like years
I'm annoyed that I still love him
That I still want him
I'm annoyed that my heart won't get on the same page as my mind
Annoyed that my couch has been a constant refuge for my behind
My mind says move on
You're better off without him
He's not your type anyway
You were generous to give him the time of day
My heart screams hold on
Like Georgia peaches, cling to him
To memories
To thoughts of what we were going to be
To what ifs and possibilities
My heart is a sucker for love
It tries to take ugly things and make them pretty
Not even divine intervention from above
Can shield me from inevitable heartbreak
If love and common sense had a tug of war
Common sense would be left in the mud
Like witches it would be burned at the stake
Heartbreak is like a constant fire burning in my chest
Slow at first
Then with a burst
Heartbreak is fueled by the pain of seeing him again
The fire can't be doused until I purge him from my system

Oiled Wings

The purging begins when he walks by
In my peripheral I catch a glimpse of him
With his new girl
That vision shatters my world inside
I force myself to hold my head high
I paint a grin on my face
Say hi and hope the façade lasts until I get out of the place
So I can go somewhere in private
And deal with the new beating
My heart is about to take

Chapter VI

EMOTIONAL

"Without purpose each day is just another day that didn't need your existence."
~ChUC

Poetry Is My Boyfriend

Like a suit and tie wrapped around bow-legs and a lean frame
He was fine
But I didn't know his name
I recall the moment that changed it all
When I first met him
In the shadows of that hole-in-the-wall
He rose up like Lazarus
And floated through the room
Like smoke from a blown out candle
Resting on a mantle
My heart rate grew quicker
Intoxicated by his lyrical liquor
He poured love's wisdom over my soul
I pulled together pieces of his words like a puzzle to make me whole
We connected intimately
He said
You don't know me
But eventually you will
I'm the real deal
An emotional goodwill pill
Let me heal you
Feed you
These dudes ain't giving you any mental stimulation
They can't find that spot
'Cause it's your brain that needs penetrating
His intellect had me on high alert
And I know he's a flirt
But could it hurt if I gave in
Poetry is my boyfriend
Searching for this feeling
I've been in and out of love
Trying to find it in somebody
I just want to spend my evenings with him
Let him fill in empty days
While sipping coffee
Or maybe enjoying a deejay
Hair wild and no makeup on my face
He's my 32 flavors
My variety

The spice in my life
I'm his lyrical wife
Emotionally spent
Legs bent, head back, smiling
He's all I need
What he gives frees me
The way he talks to me
Looks at me
Says my name
And makes love to me expressively
My love is poetry
Poetry is my boyfriend

Cool Drink

Love is like a cool drink of water on a hot summer day
Love is like the calm before a storm
Sometimes it's tested to see if it can bend and sway
Love is energy
And power
And living life purpose filled
But if you have to reason with love
And make excuses for it
Then one thing it's not, is real

Battered Woman

There are two sides to the brain of a broken woman
Hope sits on one side
Doubt sits on the other
They're like feuding sisters and brothers
Trying to out do one another
I must be crazy to think I'm special
That's the conversation that doubt has with hope
All while the woman stares in the mirror trying to find herself
Through the layers of makeup, lipstick and concealer
She's lost in a lonely wilderness where no one can hear her
Insecurity
Low self-esteem
And a battered spirit is her only company
She dabs her eyes
Cuts off her friends
And tries to recoup
She loves her kid's father
She's too scared to write "help me"
In their alphabet soup
He has a two-faced demeanor
One minute, kind
The next second, foul
She's struggling
Skating on thin ice with busted knees
Trying to get to love's heart
But with a swift kick and words full of hate
She's back to swimming in its bowels
So she shrinks down to nothing
Reverts back to going unnoticed in her mental corner
Convinced that he has all the power
The hope part of her brain doesn't understand why she just can't stay gone
Because even it doubts that the man really loves her

Micro Poem #1

He walked away with a broken stride
Following crumbs
That someone else's heart
Had left for him to find

Winter Spooning Weather

Snow falls
The wind blows
The fireplace crackles
The embers glow
There's coffee brewing in the kitchen
Potatoes, corn, green beans, and onions
Are simmering in the crockpot
His legs are wrapped around mine
My arms are tangled in his
The back of my head rests on his chest
His breath warms my ear
I love our cold lazy days together
This is good spooning weather

Cougar

He knows he's wrong for being so fine
Got my mind blown
Thinking about going home
For some lunch time loving
On the couch
In the hallway
Near the oven
It's like recreation
Physical education
Don't know who's teaching and who's learning
I don't even know his occupation
But he's got stamina and dedication
And young lungs

Up All Night

I'm craving ice cream
That's a good thing about having a boo
He can pick up a pint for you
I call – no answer
I call again – no answer
I text – no reply
I text again – no reply
Is he hurt or in trouble?
Oh God, oh God
Let him be all right
I call his mama
She hasn't seen him all night
That's funny
Earlier he said he was going by there
9 pm turns into midnight
Midnight turns into 2 am
I think about calling the police, the hospital and friends
Crazy things are going through my head
It's 4 am
The garage door opens
This fool is about to wish he was dead

Men with Sexy Hair

I inhale the scent of coconut and mango
Twirl the ends of your strength between my fingers
Oil
Twist
Shake
Retwist
Whether tied up
Pulled back
At the chin
Or free flowing at the waist
My brother
Dipped in Earth's chocolate
Birthed by Mother Nature's mother
You possess an intoxicating mojo
With those dreds you grow

What a Woman Wants

Kiss, hold, touch
Me
Treasure, cherish, adore
Me
Respect, console, move
Me
Have eyes only for me
Be in awe of me
Stand up for me
Love
Me

Confessions of a Woman Scorned

I want him to adore me
Put me first
I want him to think of me
Take care of me
I want him to provide for me
Never lie to me
I want him to get high off of me
Give me his energy
I'm not saying that he has to rip all my pain from me
But I want him to make me feel
Like he tries

Chapter VII

Sharp Edges, Smooth Curves

"Working to achieve a dream is like a 24/7 marathon but passion is your energy drink." ~ChUC

Just Do It

I am an overcomer
An achiever
A healer and a needer
I'm a realist and a dreamer
I rock Nikes and wife beaters
I run corporations
And make deals 'cause I'm a dealer
Brick by brick I've built a life
In my mind, bigger than the dynasty of the Steelers
Just a country homegirl
I stood on my own shoulders
Grew colder by opposing wind
Beating my face like a 14-drum percussion
I'm a chick under construction
No discussion about what needs to be done
I just do it

Boys to Men

-for Kaden, Rick, William, Camren

We need you to be strong men
Honorable
Better than those that came before you
We need you to be faithful, respectful and true to women
To protect them like they are your mothers
We need you to spend time cultivating greatness in yourself
And in others
We need you, young men
We need you to stand up and be responsible
Take ownership of the community around you
If the men around you are no good
Don't walk in their shoes
You are a King
Everything trifling, dishonest and lazy is beneath you
I repeat
You are a King
We need you to play when it is play time
But handle business in the meantime
We need you to be men
Before fathers hand their daughters to you
We need you to carry on a good name for our families
We need you to be all that you can
As you transition from a boy into a man

Love Jones (In the Morning)

My mind can't seem to draw the line between fact and fiction
I'm a dreamer
I'm thinking of you like it's an addiction
Your conversation is cerebral
I'm turned on by your grey matter
And the fact of the matter is I haven't even noticed your eyes
Your body is just the prize
Like Nefertiti in gold earrings
Embedded in your brain is where I wanna be
That's just the reality of my daydream
Cause I'm really digging the thought of you being here in the morning
Here with me
Cooking eggs and grits
And smelling fresh squeezed orange juice
As you caress me with the words you speak
But if I only have Tropicana
Would that be good enough
To ease your thirst from the night before
Since it came from me
Our brains connect once more for round two on the floor
And we could play scrabble
Or maybe not
You see I've got it bad
I've already played with the idea of you being here in the morning
Yesterday's blues are old news
Today's paper with all the clues are completely filled in
With my thoughts of you
Up, down and across
Your name fits perfectly
Rolls off my tongue like a saxophone's harmony
I don't know what you're trying to do
Or the plans that you have for me
But I need to let you know that I'm really feeling you
I've been sleeping on the edge of my bed to make room for you

And in my mind
I'm on the right side and you're on the left
I don't know
Maybe I'm getting ahead of myself
But I'm really digging the idea of you being here in the morning

Come Away with Me

I wash my fistful of tears down the drain
My hands must be free from old pains to catch everything love has to offer
But something deep inside of me drowns the voice that tries to scream
"I want to be the one you love"
That voice is a stranger to me
I've been trained to stay within a certain boundary mentally
Not to stray too far from what I know or to let my feelings show
Just let my brain speak
My day is filled with eight hours of complexities
So analytically I crave an uncomplicated love
But dominant is my creativity
Love will always be complicated because I am complicated
There's no thesis written about me
The love I create cannot be explained
You have to be willing to
Come away with me
To the center of my universe and see what my eyes see
Behold the clearest blue
Taste the hottest red
Touch the blackest black
For love's embrace is like holding the night sky against my skin
Like discovering a song that sings to the moon and bounces off the stars
Love pours from my heart and gets caught in my words
As comfortable as warm blankets and peppermint tea
As intricate as Mehndi
I'm just realizing how cool love can be
Where do I fit in love's history
I am the women of Sierra Leone
I am the history of Birmingham
The pyramids of Egypt
The culture of Madrid
I am the woman with two kids and no food to eat
I am the homeless in New Orleans with no shoes on their feet
I need love to understand that about me
The blood-splattered walls

That won't come clean
A sibling's crash and final curtain call
Depression, ignorance, poverty
I feel it all
So sometimes it's easier to show no feelings at all
But love, it has nothing to do with you
Please
Grab my hand and walk on the edge of my world with me
You'll understand me more once you see what I see
Come away with me

Love's Strength

My back is strong
More than enough to bear your burdens
If only for a little while

My heart is hinged
Prepared to open up fully to you
And give you all I have to offer
Plus some

My eyes have seen much mourning
Let me cry your tears
So you never know the stinging pain

Every time I blink an eye, I'm thinking of you
If your heart ever skips a beat
I wanna be so close that I can feel it, too

Cling to me
Hang on to me
Depend on me
Make plans with me
Sing songs of heartache and joy with me
And let me grow with you

Write about You

I need to write about you
Write about these feelings that I've pushed deep down inside me
Because I didn't think they really existed
Can I create a story juicer than fiction
I need to write about you
Write about love
The way I thought it was
And how I'm living it now
There's a difference
A profound difference
Love used to be thrown up hands and unspoken words
Now love is vocal
Very vocal
It talks in my ear, takes over my mind, and massages my heart
It isn't quiet
It's dynamic, heart racing and passionate
You've woven a thread of love through me
Let me sew a seed into your life
Gift my love to you
On 4x6 paper
With one-inch margins and perfect binding
Let me smother all your fears
Like a thick blanket over a grease fire
Stop, drop and roll
As I save you from life's horror story
And rewrite the ending
With me as the protagonist in your love story

Spring Love

Insatiable and unexplainable is the need for love
The need to smell it, touch it, breathe it in
Love's essence awakens me from my light sleep
I do not blink because I dare not miss it
Whether it stomps with heavy feet or enters as quietly as a whisper
I know its unique sound
I can feel it in the air
I can feel it in the room
It's home
Once I feel its presence, I am secure
I can sleep deeper
It covers me like an invisible veil of armor
Protecting me from outside elements
No, not rain, not sleet, or snow
But from the tornadic cyclones called people
Outside people who think not of my needs, its needs, our needs
Outside people who don't know what this love is about

Autumn Days

The trees are still beautiful
The brown and yellow and red leaves
Fall along the same roads I've traveled every day
For as long as I can remember
It still gets cool in December
The glow of embers from the fireplace
Warm the soles of my feet and my soul
I'm still thankful on Thanksgiving
And Christmas still comes on the 25th
The sun still shines through my window
It fills my heart with internal light and reminds me that I'm alive
No, not much has changed at all
Since you've been gone…

Micro Poem #2

No sound is sweeter
Than those three words
Vibrating off his tongue
No moment is sweeter
Than his arms wrapped around my waist
As he says them

Love, Lies & Lunacy

Check this
There are two categories of being
Those who do too much
And those who do too little
Formal education is a trip
If I didn't have good common sense
My child wouldn't know 'ish
Parents have to crack open a book just like we crack the whip
Help them read between the lines
So they don't end up on government assistance or lost on assembly lines
Rich Dad, Poor Door is a must read for the masses
Whether you're hustling products or enrolled in classes
Pride in an alma mater?
Please…
They didn't give me any accolades or degrees
I had to take 'em
But I'm not a victim
Self-pity and self-doubt, I evict 'em
My own bootstraps I pull up
Because I don't lace 'em
Still, having a lot to lose makes me follow the system
Passions dwell between reality and obscurity
My top-secret clearance is my security
So the saga continues
I'm caught up
In love, lies and lunacy

Flow Harder

Sometimes I want to flow so hard
But the words don't come
Not like I want them too
Not like I need them too
But they're there
Marinating in the back of my mind
Hiding behind all the mundane things I have to do
Stifled by the laundry I haven't done
The dinner I haven't made
The bills I haven't paid
Or the last time I got…
Well, you know
Sometimes I want to flow so hard
'Cause I have this passion
But the ideas don't come to me
Not completely
They're like half-truths and borderline lies
They can't decide what they want to be
Sometimes I want to flow so hard
But intellect gets in the way
And I think too hard
I think too long
I make a thesis out of writing a poem
Sometimes I want to flow so hard
'Cause there's a fire raging inside of me
I want to smoke out low self-esteem
Tell that little girl that she's a queen
Regardless of what's between her knees
There are too many young brothers out here dangling
I want to tell them
Ain't no future in popping folks and slanging
Sometimes I want to flow so hard
And say I know where you're going
'Cause I've been where you've been
Disappointment has been tied to my DNA
Like the ribbon at the ends of my pigtails when I was ten
The pain I felt
I didn't put in
But like the veins that run beneath my skin
It was built in

There's a truth always worthy of revealing
'Cause there's healing in empowering
So I gotta pay it forward
Reach back
Sometimes way back
And help another little girl who's struggling
So maybe she won't slit her wrist
Or pop those pills to go to sleepy land
Or dump her newborn baby in a bathroom trashcan
'Cause in the process of giving
I'm receiving a blessing

About the Author

Kimeko Farrar is an author, poet, technical writer, blogger, business owner and engineer.

She strives to find the perfect balance between accepting herself for who she is and pushing past her comfort zone to reach her full potential. She founded the Chick Under Construction platform because she believes that every woman deserves encouragement to build a life based on purpose. Chick Under Construction's focus is to support women in achieving their dreams and living a life that inspires others. Kimeko is also the owner of ChUC, ink, which is a multi-faceted company that caters to the bold, expressive and creative dreamer. ChUC, ink publishes fiction and non-fiction literature, designs chic apparel, and embraces natural hair and fitness.

Kimeko was a contributing author in the anthologies; *Oil and Water and Other Things that Don't Mix* (2010) and *She Speaks* (2012).

Connect with Kimeko

www.facebook.com/KIMEKO.FARRAR

www.facebook.com/CHUCInk

www.kimekofarrar.com

www.youtube.com/meko1908

Instagram & Twitter: Kimeko Farrar

ChUC, ink

For information about special discounts for bulk purchases or bringing the author to your live event, please contact ChUC, ink at kimeko@kimekofarrar.com

Thanks to readers, buyers and contributors of this book. I love you all! ~ Kimeko

www.ingramcontent.com/pod-product-compliance
Lightning Source LLC
LaVergne TN
LVHW052254070426
835507LV00035B/2903